Francis Frith's
THE ISLE OF WIGHT

PHOTOGRAPHIC MEMORIES

Francis Frith's
THE ISLE OF WIGHT

◆

John Bainbridge

First published in the United Kingdom in 2000 by
Frith Book Company Ltd

ISBN 1-85937-114-0
Reprinted in hardback 2001

Paperback Edition 2001
1-85937-429-8
Reprinted in paperback 2003
1-85937-429-8

British Library Cataloguing in Publication Data

The Isle of Wight
John Bainbridge
ISBN 1-85937-429-8

Frith Book Company Ltd
Frith's Barn, Teffont,
Salisbury, Wiltshire SP3 5QP
Tel: +44 (0) 1722 716 376
Email:
info@frithbook.co.uk

Front Cover: **SHANKLIN**, *The Stagecoaches 1913* 66211a

Frontispiece: **COWES**, *Victoria Pier 1923* 74750

*The colour-tinting is for illustrative purposes only,
and is not intended to be historically accurate*

Printed and bound in Great Britain

CONTENTS

FRANCIS FRITH: *Victorian Pioneer*

FRANCIS FRITH, Victorian founder of the world-famous photographic archive, was a complex and multitudinous man. A devout Quaker and a highly successful Victorian businessman, he was both philosophic by nature and pioneering in outlook.

By 1855 Francis Frith had already established a wholesale grocery business in Liverpool, and sold it for the astonishing sum of £200,000, which is the equivalent today of over £15,000,000. Now a very rich man, he was able to indulge his passion for travel. As a child he had pored over travel books written by early explorers, and his fancy and imagination had been stirred by family holidays to the sublime mountain regions of Wales and Scotland. 'What lands of spirit-stirring and enriching scenes and places!' he had written. He was to return to these scenes of grandeur in later years to 'recapture the thousands of vivid and tender memories', but with a different purpose. Now in his thirties, and captivated by the new science of photography, Frith set out on a series of pioneering journeys to the Nile regions that occupied him from 1856 until 1860.

INTRIGUE AND ADVENTURE

He took with him on his travels a specially-designed wicker carriage that acted as both dark-room and sleeping chamber. These far-flung journeys were packed with intrigue and adventure. In his life story, written when he was sixty-three, Frith tells of being held captive by bandits, and of fighting 'an awful midnight battle to the very point of surrender with a deadly pack of hungry, wild dogs'. Sporting flowing Arab costume, Frith arrived at Akaba by camel seventy years before Lawrence, where he encountered 'desert princes and rival sheikhs, blazing with jewel-hilted swords'.

During these extraordinary adventures he was assiduously exploring the desert regions bordering the Nile and patiently recording the antiquities and peoples with his camera. He was the first photographer to venture beyond the sixth cataract. Africa was still the mysterious 'Dark Continent', and Stanley and Livingstone's historic meeting was a decade into the future. The conditions for picture taking confound belief. He laboured for hours in his wicker dark-room in the sweltering heat of the desert, while the volatile chemicals fizzed dangerously in their trays. Often he was forced to work in remote tombs and caves

where conditions were cooler. Back in London he exhibited his photographs and was 'rapturously cheered' by members of the Royal Society. His reputation as a photographer was made overnight. An eminent modern historian has likened their impact on the population of the time to that on our own generation of the first photographs taken on the surface of the moon.

VENTURE OF A LIFE-TIME

Characteristically, Frith quickly spotted the opportunity to create a new business as a specialist publisher of photographs. He lived in an era of immense and sometimes violent change. For the poor in the early part of Victoria's reign work was a drudge and the hours long, and people had precious little free time to enjoy themselves.

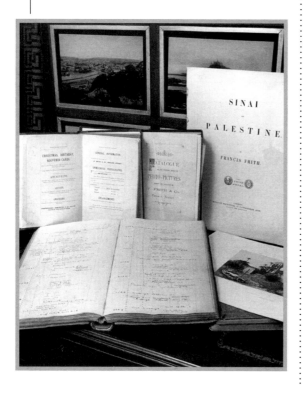

Most had no transport other than a cart or gig at their disposal, and had not travelled far beyond the boundaries of their own town or village. However, by the 1870s, the railways had threaded their way across the country, and Bank Holidays and half-day Saturdays had been made obligatory by Act of Parliament. All of a sudden the ordinary working man and his family were able to enjoy days out and see a little more of the world.

With characteristic business acumen, Francis Frith foresaw that these new tourists would enjoy having souvenirs to commemorate their days out. In 1860 he married Mary Ann Rosling and set out with the intention of photographing every city, town and village in Britain. For the next thirty years he travelled the country by train and by pony and trap, producing fine photographs of seaside resorts and beauty spots that were keenly bought by millions of Victorians. These prints were painstakingly pasted into family albums and pored over during the dark nights of winter, rekindling precious memories of summer excursions.

THE RISE OF FRITH & CO

Frith's studio was soon supplying retail shops all over the country. To meet the demand he gathered about him a small team of photographers, and published the work of independent artist-photographers of the calibre of Roger Fenton and Francis Bedford. In order to gain some understanding of the scale of Frith's business one only has to look at the catalogue issued by Frith & Co in 1886: it runs to some 670

pages, listing not only many thousands of views of the British Isles but also many photographs of most European countries, and China, Japan, the USA and Canada – note the sample page shown above from the hand-written *Frith & Co* ledgers detailing pictures taken. By 1890 Frith had created the greatest specialist photographic publishing company in the world, with over 2,000 outlets – more than the combined number that Boots and WH Smith have today! The picture on the right shows the *Frith & Co* display board at Ingleton in the Yorkshire Dales (left of window). Beautifully constructed with a mahogany frame and gilt inserts, it could display up to a dozen local scenes.

POSTCARD BONANZA

◆ ◆

The ever-popular holiday postcard we know today took many years to develop. In 1870 the Post Office issued the first plain cards, with a pre-printed stamp on one face. In 1894 they allowed other publishers' cards to be sent through the mail with an attached adhesive halfpenny stamp. Demand grew rapidly, and in 1895 a new size of postcard was permitted called the

court card, but there was little room for illustration. In 1899, a year after Frith's death, a new card measuring 5.5 x 3.5 inches became the standard format, but it was not until 1902 that the divided back came into being, with address and message on one face and a full-size illustration on the other. *Frith & Co* were in the vanguard of postcard development, and Frith's sons Eustace and Cyril continued their father's monumental task, expanding the number of views offered to the public and recording more and more places in Britain, as the coasts and countryside were opened up to mass travel.

Francis Frith died in 1898 at his villa in Cannes, his great project still growing. The archive he created continued in business for another seventy years. By 1970 it contained over a third of a million pictures of 7,000 cities, towns and villages. The massive photographic record Frith has left to us stands as a living monument to a special and very remarkable man.

Frith's Archive: *A Unique Legacy*

FRANCIS FRITH'S legacy to us today is of immense significance and value, for the magnificent archive of evocative photographs he created provides a unique record of change in 7,000 cities, towns and villages throughout Britain over a century and more. Frith and his fellow studio photographers revisited locations many times down the years to update their views, compiling for us an enthralling and colourful pageant of British life and character.

We tend to think of Frith's sepia views of Britain as nostalgic, for most of us use them to conjure up memories of places in our own lives with which we have family associations. It often makes us forget that to Francis Frith they were records of daily life as it was actually being lived in the cities, towns and villages of his day. The Victorian age was one of great and often bewildering change for ordinary people, and though the pictures evoke an impression of slower times, life was as busy and hectic as it is today.

We are fortunate that Frith was a photographer of the people, dedicated to recording the minutiae of everyday life. For it is this sheer wealth of visual data, the painstaking chronicle of changes in dress, transport, street layouts, buildings, housing, engineering and landscape that captivates us so much today. His remarkable images offer us a powerful link with the past and with the lives of our ancestors.

TODAY'S TECHNOLOGY

Computers have now made it possible for Frith's many thousands of images to be accessed almost instantly. In the Frith archive today, each photograph is carefully 'digitised' then stored on a CD Rom. Frith archivists can locate a single photograph amongst thousands within seconds. Views can be catalogued and sorted under a variety of categories of place and content to the immediate benefit of researchers. Inexpensive reference prints can be created for them at the touch of a mouse button, and a wide range of books and other printed materials assembled and published for a wider, more general readership. The day-to-day workings of the archive are very different from how they were in Francis Frith's

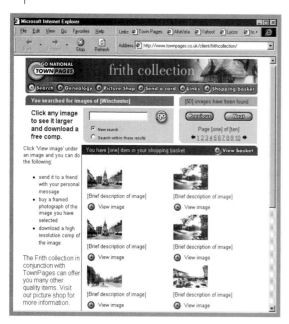

See Frith at www. frithbook.co.uk

time: imagine the herculean task of sorting through eleven tons of glass negatives as Frith had to do to locate a particular sequence of pictures! Yet the archive still prides itself on maintaining the same high standards of excellence laid down by Francis Frith, including the painstaking cataloguing and indexing of every view.

It is curious to reflect on how the internet now allows researchers in America and elsewhere greater instant access to the archive than Frith himself ever enjoyed. Many thousands of individual views can be called up on screen within seconds on one of the Frith internet sites, enabling people living continents away to revisit the streets of their ancestral home town, or view places in Britain where they have enjoyed holidays. Many overseas researchers welcome the chance to view special theme selections, such as transport, sports, costume and ancient monuments.

We are certain that Francis Frith would have heartily approved of these modern developments, for he himself was always working at the very limits of Victorian photographic technology.

THE VALUE OF THE ARCHIVE TODAY

Because of the benefits brought by the computer, Frith's images are increasingly studied by social historians, by researchers into genealogy and ancestory, by architects, town planners, and by teachers and schoolchildren involved in local history projects. In addition, the archive offers every one of us a unique opportunity to examine the places where we and our families have lived

and worked down the years. Immensely successful in Frith's own era, the archive is now, a century and more on, entering a new phase of popularity.

THE PAST IN TUNE WITH THE FUTURE

Historians consider the Francis Frith Collection to be of prime national importance. It is the only archive of its kind remaining in private ownership and has been valued at a million pounds. However, this figure is now rapidly increasing as digital technology enables more and more people around the world to enjoy its benefits.

Francis Frith's archive is now housed in an historic timber barn in the beautiful village of Teffont in Wiltshire. Its founder would not recognize the archive office as it is today. In place of the many thousands of dusty boxes containing glass plate negatives and an all-pervading odour of photographic chemicals, there are now ranks of computer screens. He would be amazed to watch his images travelling round the world at unimaginable speeds through network and internet lines.

The archive's future is both bright and exciting. Francis Frith, with his unshakeable belief in making photographs available to the greatest number of people, would undoubtedly approve of what is being done today with his lifetime's work. His photographs, depicting our shared past, are now bringing pleasure and enlightenment to millions around the world a century and more after his death.

THE ISLE OF WIGHT – *An Introduction*

Early Island History

The presence of ancient monuments - and the barrows on the high downlands across the central belt of the island, the burial mounds of some of our most distant ancestors - show us that the Isle of Wight was inhabited long before the Roman legions arrived during the Emperor Claudius' invasion of England in AD 43. The Roman Empire kept possession of the island, known to them as Vecta or Vectis, until AD 530, when the Saxons swept in from the east and began to colonise, establishing a stronghold at Carisbrooke and giving new names to a score of older settlements.

Much of the history of the past two millennia has been troubled and violent, and even this attractive and productive island did not escape the worst excesses of man's wars. From the Iron Age to the 20th century the Isle of Wight - so close to foreign shores - has known invasion and attack. Iron Age tribes battled with their enemies there and probably resisted the Roman invaders. The Saxon warlord Cedric and his hordes raged across the island, and the internecine warfare which followed during the Anglo-Saxon period brought more misery to this beautiful wooded island in the English Channel. No sooner were the Anglo-Saxons peacefully working the land than Danish raiders arrived to raid and plunder. They were soon fought off by Saxon settlers, who had not embraced their farming pursuits so much that they had forgotten how to fight.

At the Norman Conquest William Fitz-Osborne fortified Carisbrooke yet again, on behalf of his kinsman the new King of England. After this subjugation the island bore no more invasions, but was constantly in peril from channel raids by the French, including prolonged attacks on several occasions when its towns were put to fire and sword. Its position in England's front line has meant that the Isle of Wight has faced danger in recent times as well as at the dawn of history. In 1940 the island was one of the first parts of Britain to be bombed during the Battle of Britain, as the Luftwaffe attempted to destroy important radar stations near Ventnor.

As with so many parts of England, the past is writ plain across the landscape; interpreting this evidence adds to the joys of a visit to the island, for history can be a matter of creativity as well as conflict. Those who wish to explore the Isle of Wight's heritage do not have to search for very long for reminders of its crowded history, for a great profusion of antiquities remain to be examined. There are Roman villas, civilised with evidence of central heating, from the more peaceful years of that occupation; exquisite Norman and Early English churches; and fortifications from most of the past thousand years - from the mighty Carisbrooke Castle to the blockhouse forts of Henry VIII, and from Victorian defences to the concrete bunkers of the Second World War.

Queen Victoria made this island both her own and a fashionable destination for millions of her subjects. As heir to the throne, the Princess Alexandrina Victoria had spent some time staying with her mother on the island, playing on the seashore at East Cowes, gathering seaweeds and shells in much the same way as any other little girl at the seaside. She never forgot the experience. After her marriage to Prince Albert she bought Osborne House, using it as her favoured winter retreat until the very end of her life, and dying there in January 1901.

No one should underestimate the importance of this royal patronage to the Isle of Wight. Its consequences were far reaching and changed the way of life on the island for ever. Fishing villages became residential towns and important resorts. The population soared and towns enjoyed a housing boom as residences and hotels were built to cater for the increased demand for homes and holiday accommodation. Locals, who might otherwise have found employment in farming and fishing, found themselves instead the pioneer workers of a burgeoning tourist industry.

The Holiday Island

◆◆

There are few English journeys more delightful than to take a ferry from one of the Hampshire ports across to the Isle of Wight, with its mild climate, luxuriant vegetation and long and evident history. The island ahead has often been compared to a beautiful tapes-

cycles, beachcombs or bathes, the island and its waters offer a multitude of delights.

The island, for that is usually how residents refer to the place, is small in comparison with most English counties, measuring some 23 miles by 13 miles. In olden times the Isle of Wight was heavily wooded. It is thought that many of these old forests were taken down to

try by those who have approached on fine summer days. The beautiful colour of the cliffs, the patchwork fields, deep green woods and brightly-coloured sails in the harbours and channels more than justify this description. Those who visit the island once invariably fall in love with it and return again and again, for there is far too much to seek out and admire in one visit. The Isle of Wight has enough to fascinate the tourist interested in geology, archaeology, history, and nature. For the active participant who sails or walks,

provide wood for the ships built at neighbouring ports such as Portsmouth and Southampton. What has been left is a verdant landscape of fields and hedgerows, high downlands, deep wooded valleys and chines. The coastal scenery is some of the best in England.

The towns of the island grew for functional purposes, making little concession to the demands of increasing tourism until quite late in the day. Newport is, despite its name, a very ancient port and the old capital of the island. Standing at the estuary of the Medina, that lengthy river that almost divides the island, Newport is a good central base for an exploration of this fascinating land. Shanklin and Sandown, those twin towns connected by the long promenade running around a goodly stretch of Shanklin Bay, are something approaching traditional holiday resorts, boosted in their fortunes by some of the safest bathing on the Isle of Wight. Cowes and Yarmouth flourished both as the entry ports to the island and as important yachting centres. Ryde and Ventnor are seaside towns, the first an entry port with its unique railway pier to welcome tens of thousands of tourists every year; the latter an ideal base for exploring the exciting southern coastline. But before the advent of popular tourism, and that was a very Victorian development on the Isle of Wight, these towns served only the traditional trades of fishing and farming.

So sudden was this tourist phenomenon that native islanders seemed to experience difficulties coming to terms with the massive influx of well-to-do Victorian visitors. At least one early guidebook writer perceived some resentment from the local population, finding them churlish and stand-offish towards the 'overner' as incomers were called. But it seems as if this resistance to change was futile as the locals were overwhelmed by those who followed in the Queen Victoria's footsteps. A R Hope Moncrieff, that most acerbic of Victorian commentators, noted that 'a great part of the upper class of the inhabitants, indeed, now consists of well-to-do strangers who have settled in the island, attracted by its various amenities, while the sons of the soil have too large experience of 'overners' in the relation of profitable guests, to retain any sus-

picious dislike of their incursions'. Patronising, but probably true! Though Hope Moncrieff did add the caution that 'a certain insular independence, not to say rudeness, may still be observed occasionally in the manner of the local youth towards strangers'. Tourists today, happily, receive a much warmer welcome.

Looking closely at these photographs it is interesting to note just how every aspect of the island seems to have been geared towards tourism. Not that older industries declined entirely, even in the Isle of Wight's Victorian heyday - or indeed today. Fishing boats continue to work from seaside harbours, farming still flourishes on the island's best pastoral fields and sheep graze the high downlands. But by the time that Frith and his family turned their attentions to the Isle of Wight, tourism was certainly the dominant industry. We see here how the visitors were brought across the water, where they stayed on their arrival, the beaches where they bathed, the sea walls and piers where they promenaded and the tourist traps that just had to be visited.

Not that tourism was new to southern England. Holiday resorts had prospered on the south coast for a century before Victoria arrived at Osborne House. But seldom before had tourists had an opportunity to take over such a vast and at the same time contained landscape. That this happened without seriously compromising the very beauty that all of these tourists came to see is surely a credit not only to those who lived and worked on the island during those important formative years, but to those who are its custodians today.

ALUM BAY, THE BEACH c1955 A41008
The coloured cliffs of Alum Bay are one of the most enduring sights on the Isle of Wight as far as visitors are concerned. Blue, red, yellow, grey, white and black are the shades of the strata here, and the location is as wild and beautiful as anywhere in England.

BEMBRIDGE, THE VILLAGE 1923 74681
Bembridge, the easternmost settlement on the Isle of Wight, became popular in late-Victorian times as a centre for golf, being the headquarters of the Isle of Wight Golf Club. Early golfers found they had to take a ferry to the links on the far side of Brading Harbour if they wanted a game.

BEMBRIDGE, THE SLIPWAY C1955 B64004

Bembridge is surrounded by attractive and tranquil scenery. Its harbour has always been a place to pass a lazy afternoon and eat snacks as you watch the boats. Riley's Pantry, seen here on the right, advertises fresh lobster sandwiches at 6d each. Such is the demand for eating places that the old lifeboat house opposite has also been converted into a cafe.

BEMBRIDGE, THE HUTS C1955 B64005

A closer view of the group in the previous photograph reveals them relaxing on the slipway. The huts beyond show the popularity of this part of the island for bathing; there are pleasant stretches of sand among the shingle of the beach.

BEMBRIDGE, HIGH STREET c1955 B64020

BEMBRIDGE
High Street c1955
Bembridge is the location of a famous public school founded in the first half of the 20th century by the spirited Mr Whitehouse. This gentleman was a fervent admirer of both the art-critic John Ruskin and the polar explorer Nansen, using their artistic and adventurous philosophies as the inspiration for his teaching.

◆

BEMBRIDGE
High Street c1955
Bembridge's shops have always been functional, serving the simple needs of residents and tourists alike. A railway arrived nearby in Victoria's reign, and accommodation was provided in guest houses and hotels, some offering 'special terms to golfers'.

BEMBRIDGE, HIGH STREET c1955 B64022

BEMBRIDGE, HIGH STREET c1955 B64034

This eastern end of the Isle of Wight enjoys a milder climate than the busy towns on the north coast, and health-conscious early visitors came for the quality of the air. Its purity and warmth has encouraged a variety of plants to flourish, making Bembridge a favoured centre for botanical studies.

BEMBRIDGE, THE YACHT CLUB c1955 B64025

Most people associate the Isle of Wight with sailing, but few think beyond major resorts such as Cowes for the activity. The smaller harbours support their yacht clubs as well, and are often better places for the beginner to learn to sail.

BEMBRIDGE
The Old Windmill c1955
This excellent study of the old windmill at Bembridge reminds us that such structures were once common across England, though few survive in working condition; the majority have been converted into homes or, worse, demolished.

◆

BINSTEAD
The Village c1955
Situated on the high road between Cowes and Ryde, Binstead has views across the Solent to Spithead. The nearby quarries - and much of Binstead's villagers must have worked in them when they were active - provided the stone for the cathedrals at Chichester and Winchester.

BEMBRIDGE, THE OLD WINDMILL C1955 B64301

BINSTEAD, THE VILLAGE C1955 B772003

BINSTEAD, THE CHURCH c1955 B772001

Binstead's original Norman church was built under the instructions of the abbot of nearby Quarr Abbey, who did not wish the peasants of Binstead to worship in his own chapels. Much of the building is now a Victorian rebuilding, though there are a few remnants of the original church.

BINSTEAD, THE FORGE c1955 B772010

The area around Binstead, particularly the waste tips of the old quarries, is a rich source of supply for the fossil-hunter. Freshwater shell fossils, the fruits of ancient trees, and the fossilised remains of mammals can all be discovered.

BINSTEAD, THE VILLAGE c1955 B772021
The Victorian poet Horace Smith wrote these lines on leaving the village: 'Farewell, sweet Binstead! Take a fond farewell/From one unused to sight of woods and trees,/ Amid the strife of cities doomed to dwell,/Yet roused to ecstasy by scenes like these;/Who could for ever sit beneath thy trees,/Inhaling fragrance from the flowery dell'.

BLACKGANG CHINE, VIEW FROM THE OBSERVATORY c1955 B113051
The great chasm of Blackgang Chine was an early tourist attraction on the Isle of Wight, with its dramatic waterfall and eroded colourful cliffs. The waves of the sea echo along the Chine on wilder days, whilst much of the island's southern coastline can be seen from the Observatory.

BLACKGANG CHINE, THE GARDENS c1955 B113035
Entry to the chasm was relatively expensive in Victorian times. One guidebook writer noted that 'entrance to the Chine is through a bazaar, where one must either make a purchase or pay sixpence before he descends to this great chasm, echoing the ocean waves that break on the beach below'.

BONCHURCH, THE POND 1890 26151
Bonchurch is a charming suburb of Ventnor, its rich plant life a joy to behold. The pond, a favourite scene for the Victorian visitor, was overhung with huge arbutus trees, scarlet geraniums, and fuchsias with trunks as thick as a man's wrist.

BONCHURCH, THE VILLAGE AND THE POST OFFICE 1934 86287
Bonchurch stands on the steep slopes of St Boniface Down. Both the hillside and village are named after the Devon-born churchman who brought Christianity to Germany. The original Saxon church may have been founded by the saint before he went abroad.

BONCHURCH
Jacob's Ladder 1918
One early visitor to Bonchurch was Alfred, Lord Tennyson, who loved the local walks. Not all of his perambulations were without incident. On one occasion the poet was mobbed by a group of lady fans, who cut his hat to pieces as souvenirs.

BONCHURCH
The Village c1955
Buried in the churchyard lies the poet and intellectual rebel Algernon Charles Swinburne, who died in 1909. Swinburne's happier lyrics may have been inspired by his frequent visits to the Isle of Wight, though the greater body of his work has a bleakness and pessimism that seems alien to this beautiful and inspiring locality.

BONCHURCH, JACOB'S LADDER 1918 68282

BONCHURCH, THE VILLAGE C1955 B139014

BONCHURCH, THE POND AND THE CAFE c1955 B139106

This later view of the pond is worth comparing to the earlier photograph of the same scene. Horses have given way to the ubiquitous motor car, and the village is catering for the car-borne tourist. But the pond and the wooded nooks around Bonchurch are as great an attraction as they were for the Victorian visitor.

BONCHURCH, THE BEACH c1955 B139084

The shingly and sandy beaches of Bonchurch have always drawn a great number of bathers, and can get crowded on hot summer days. Apart from visitors staying in the villages, these beaches attract others from Ventnor, a short stroll away.

BONCHURCH
The Beach c1955

Bonchurch became a fashionable place to live during Queen Victoria's reign. Many large houses from that period are scattered around the village and near to the sea. Most have extensive gardens of great beauty. By the next century some had been converted into hotels providing seaside holidays for affluent post-war visitors.

BRADING
The Village 1923

Brading is one of the oldest towns on the Isle of Wight, once returning two members to Parliament. People have lived in this locality for a long time - not far away is a fine example of a Roman villa, with a pavement showing Orpheus playing a lute and surrounded by animals.

BONCHURCH, THE BEACH c1955 B139116

BRADING, THE VILLAGE 1923 74688

BRADING, OLD COTTAGES c1955 B175002
At the beginning of the 19th century Brading's curate was Legh Richmond, whose moral tale 'The Annals of the Poor' and other rural stories enjoyed a large readership. Richmond worked hard for the local community, and his tales incorporated and made famous several real-life residents of the town.

BRADING, HIGH STREET c1955 B175003
During a French attack on England in 1545, a large fleet of warships anchored off Brading harbour in the hope that the English fleet could be lured out of Portsmouth. When the English vessels failed to appear, French troops landed on the island, burning and looting, and were resisted only by the islanders who inflicted heavy casualties on the invaders.

BRADING
The Church c1955
Brading church is mostly Norman in design, though with some traces of an even older building. There are some beautiful epitaphs to be found in the churchyard, including one beginning 'Forgive, blest shade, the tributary tear', which was set to music by Dr Calcutt in the 19th century.

BRADING
High Street c1955
There are some fine memorials within the church, notably those of the Oglander family, who had held land nearby since the Norman Conquest. Sir John Oglander, who died in 1655, wrote an early history of the Isle of Wight.

BRADING, THE CHURCH c1955 B175004

BRADING, HIGH STREET c1955 B175009

BRADING, THE BULL RING c1955 B175010

Brading's Bull Ring is a legacy of the barbaric tradition of bull-baiting, where a tethered animal would be attacked by a succession of dogs. All that remains is a wide open space and the tethering ring.

BRADING, HIGH STREET c1955 B175024

Not far away from the Bull Ring are displayed the town stocks and whipping post. Early inhabitants of the High Street faced a range of fierce punishments if they transgressed the law, including flogging, mutilation and death by hanging.

BRADING, HIGH STREET c1965 B175038
This lovely old building, the town museum and waxworks when this photograph was taken, adorns Brading High Street. Note the early appearance of double yellow lines prohibiting car parking.

BRIGHSTONE, THE VILLAGE c1955 B543003
Thomas Ken, who was rector of Brighstone before becoming Bishop of Winchester, ministered to Charles II as he lay dying; accompanied Charles' illegitimate son the Duke of Monmouth on his way to the block; and was one of the Seven Bishops who helped secure the accession of William of Orange.

CALBOURNE, WINKLE STREET c1955 C439009

The pretty village of Calbourne lies among the downlands of the Isle of Wight. Its lovely Early English church boasts many fine monuments and is among the oldest on the island. The long line of cottages in Winkle Street overlooks a delightful babbling brook.

CARISBROOKE, CASTLE HILL 1908 60509

Carisbrooke Castle stands on a high mound, dominating the town below. The site may have been fortified as long ago as Roman times, though much of today's castle dates back to the Norman period with later additions. The foundations for the castle were laid by William Fitz-Osborne, a kinsman of the Conqueror.

CARISBROOKE, FROM THE CASTLE c1955 C26042
King Charles I was held prisoner at Carisbrooke after the Civil War. A window through which he attempted to escape is still shown to visitors. His daughter Elizabeth Stuart died aged fourteen in the castle, soon after her father's execution.

CARISBROOKE, HIGH STREET c1955 C26001
Carisbrooke's church, once part of a larger priory, has a fine and dominant perpendicular tower. The original church and priory were probably founded by William Fitz-Osborne and date back to the same period as the castle.

CARISBROOKE, THE VILLAGE c1955 C26007
Among the many monuments within the church is the tomb of Lady Dorothy Wadham, the sister of Queen Jane Seymour. The nearby epitaph to Charles Dixon, a local blacksmith, ends with the lines 'My fire-dried corpse here lies at rest, My soul, snake-like, soars to be blest'.

CARISBROOKE, HIGH STREET c1955 C26004
Carisbrooke's dramatic castle, rich in history, made the town a popular tourist attraction with early visitors, including the poet Tennyson, who may have incorporated aspects of the castle into his romantic verse.

CARISBROOKE, THE VILLAGE c1955 C26005
A Roman villa was unearthed at Carisbrooke in 1859 and found to cover an area of some 120 feet by 55 feet. The excavations revealed a building of several rooms, including a semi-circular bath and a central heating system.

CARISBROOKE
Castle Street c1955

The water in the castle's deep well was drawn for centuries by the use of donkey labour, a fresh supply being essential in times of siege. Visitors in more peaceful times have had the happier choice of several tea rooms when in need of refreshment.

CARISBROOKE
Main Street c1955

Victorian visitors had a number of inns to choose from when seeking sustenance in the town, some acting as fully-fledged hotels. A Victorian guidebook noted that 'the coach excursionist will be saved the trouble of choosing his quarters, as the coaches usually set him down at the Carisbrooke Castle or the Eight Bells'.

CARISBROOKE, CASTLE STREET c1955 C26006

CARISBROOKE, MAIN STREET c1955 C26032

COLWELL BAY, THE FRONT c1955 C452001
Colwell Bay, just west of Yarmouth, has a good mile of sand sheltered by the low cliffs behind. Albert Fort, on the headland at one end of the bay, was built to guard the strategically important waters of the Solent.

COWES, THE ESPLANADE c1871 5749
The two Cowes, situated on the west and east banks of the River Medina, are famous throughout the world as a centre for yachting and as the home port of the Royal Yacht Squadron. Many visitors gain their first impressions of the Isle of Wight as they land by ferry from Southampton.

COWES, THE PIER 1893 32838
Cowes harbour is a fine natural anchorage which has been appreciated by sailors for centuries. The early local historian Sir John Oglander remarked that he saw some 300 ships riding at anchor there in 1620.

COWES, VICTORIA PIER 1908 60491

Cowes has always been more popular as a touring base than as a traditional seaside resort, though one rhymester tried to remedy the situation in 1760 when he wrote 'No more to foreign baths shall Britons roam, But plunge at Cowes, and find rich health at home!'

COWES, THE ESPLANADE 1913 66311

Thomas Arnold, the headmaster of Rugby School, immortalised in 'Tom Brown's Schooldays', was born at Cowes in 1796. Arnold probably did more than most to shape the popular perception of Victorian values.

COWES, FLOATING BRIDGE 1913 66313
This ferry, known as a chain ferry or floating bridge, is the means of crossing the long inlet of the Medina. The alternative is a lengthy detour inland as far as Newport.

COWES, VIEW FROM THE PIER 1927 80463

Hotels and yacht chandlers line the seashore at Cowes. The town's importance as a centre for yachting, and the close proximity of Queen Victoria's home Osborne House, made Cowes most fashionable in the 19th century. A large number of hotels were built to cater for the increased number of tourists.

COWES, OLD HOUSES 1927 80465

King Henry VIII built two defensive castles on either side of the Medina to protect the entrance to the older harbour at Newport. An ancient rhyme runs: 'The two great Cows that in loud thunder roar, This on the eastern, that the western shore, Where Newport enters stately Wight'".

COWES, VICTORIA PIER 1923 74750
This view over Victoria Pier gives a good idea of the
variety of ships and smaller boats that could be seen
sailing off Cowes on an average day between the wars.

COWES, THE QUEEN MARY c1955 C173004
The great liner Queen Mary was a regular sight across the waters of Cowes Roads, leaving and entering Southampton. This stretch of water has seen the departure of many famous vessels and armadas, including Henry V's expedition to Harfleur, Nelson's Victory and the D-Day invasion fleet.

COWES, WATCHING THE RACING 1933 85896
A yachting regatta first took place off Cowes in 1776. The town's yacht club became the Royal Yacht Club in 1820 on the accession of George IV, a notable member. In 1933 the club became the prestigious Royal Yacht Squadron.

EAST COWES, SAUNDERS ROE SEAPLANE BASE c1955 E139005
A flying boat undergoes repair at West Cowes looking across to the famous Saunders Roe yards at East Cowes. The long arm of the Medina estuary provided good shelter for seaplanes and was used for this purpose from the First World War onwards.

COWES, A FLYING BOAT c1955 C173016

COWES
A Flying Boat c1955
A flying boat rests on the calm waters of the Medina, in the peaceful days of the 1950s. A decade earlier the Isle of Wight had known the hostile use of air-power, being one of the first areas to be bombed during the Battle of Britain.

COWES
The Hovercraft c1965
An early hovercraft taking passengers across the Solent. Ten years before, Cockerell's prototype hovercraft had made its first test runs off the mouth of the Medina.

COWES, THE HOVERCRAFT c1965 C173090

COWES, BATH ROAD c1955 C173001

Some attempt was made in Georgian times to turn Cowes into a fashionable watering place. It never happened, because of the limited suitability of the sea bathing available.

COWES, THE PROMENADE c1955 C173010

Bathing is possible along some of the beaches at Cowes, particularly at Gurnard Bay. However, the currents are strong and the shoreline shelves steeply. Cowes' reputation as a yachting paradise overwhelmed all real attempts to open the town up as a simple holiday resort.

COWES, NORTHWOOD HOUSE c1955 C173029

Northwood House was the home of Tennyson's friend William George Ward in the 19th century. The poet and Ward would often stroll around Northwood's exquisite gardens. After his friend's death Tennyson wrote: 'Farewell, whose living like I shall not find, My friend, the most unworldly of mankind'.

COWES, THE VECTA c1955 C173032

Twenty-one cannons, once the guns of the sailing ship Royal Adelaide, are used to start the yachting races during Cowes Week every August. In the background a ferry heads into port.

COWES, HIGH STREET c1955 C173002
Queen Victoria's residence at nearby Osborne House brought thousands of curious visitors and much prosperity
to the Isle of Wight. Many eminent citizens followed her example and built homes nearby. The shops in Cowes
shared in this economic good fortune.

COWES, HIGH STREET c1955 C173039

The 17th-century historian Sir John Oglander remarked in his famous work that 'I knew when there were not three or four houses at Cowes'. By the time this photograph was taken, Cowes was one of the most populated sites on the island.

COWES, HIGH STREET c1955 C173046

The narrow streets of Cowes are typical of many southern English coastal towns, designed for use rather than ornament. As befits a sailing town, a number of shops have always been given over to yacht chandlery and provisions.

EAST COWES, THE FLOATING BRIDGE c1955 E139007
The floating bridge crossed the Medina from West to East Cowes. Notice the wharves and docks in the background. Some of the wooden battleships of Nelson's navy were built at the waterline of East Cowes. During the world wars of the 20th century the tradition continued, and many destroyers and smaller naval vessels were constructed there.

EAST COWES, THE DOCKYARD c1955 E139004
East Cowes was once the more important of the two towns, though it has now been eclipsed by the sprawling town on the opposite side of the Medina. Its old Tudor fortress has long since disappeared, though the boyhood home of Dr Thomas Arnold remains.

EAST COWES
Street Scene c1955

Queen Victoria first stayed on the Isle of Wight at Norris Castle, during the reign of her uncle William IV. Years later, when she was monarch herself, she bought Osborne House not far away. It is said that when she was a young girl she collected rare varieties of seaweed on the beaches around East Cowes, which she presented to her friend Maria da Gloria, girl-queen of Portugal.

◆

FRESHWATER BAY
The Village 1923

Freshwater gets its name from the supply of pure clean water rising so near to the sea. It now gives its name to a district at the southwestern end of the Isle of Wight, from the village itself, a couple of miles inland, to the popular Freshwater Bay on the south coast.

EAST COWES, STREET SCENE c1955 E139058

FRESHWATER BAY, THE VILLAGE 1923 74727

FRESHWATER, GENERAL VIEW C1955 F49014

A little way back from Freshwater Bay is the former home of the poet Tennyson, who loved the place but hated the constant procession of visitors. The high cliffs and startling rock formations - perhaps the most dramatic scenery on the Isle of Wight after The Needles - brings visitors back again and again.

FRESHWATER, THE ESPLANADE C1955 F49020

The esplanade at Freshwater Bay is a favourite place to stroll on long summer days, though in the winter it serves as a sturdy defence against wild weather and channel gales. A few hotels line the sea front, with the rest of the village a little way inland.

FRESHWATER, THE BEACH c1965 F49005
Tennyson's gaunt figure could often be seen walking the beach in Victorian times. He described the scene in verse: 'Groves of pine on either hand To break the blast of winter, stand; And further on, the heavy channel Tumbles a breaker on chalk and sand'.

LIMERSTONE, THE VILLAGE c1955 B543005
A couple of miles away at Brighstone Down are ancient reminders of human life on the island - twelve Bronze Age burial mounds.

NEWCHURCH, THE POINTER INN AND THE CHURCH c1955 N113003
Despite its name, Newchurch is one of the oldest parishes on the Isle of Wight, and once included Ryde and Ventnor within its bounds. The church dates back to the Norman Conquest, though it contains additions from most historic periods.

NEWCHURCH, THE VILLAGE c1955 N113007
Newchurch was the home of Richard Forward, who served as its schoolmaster for 53 years. The epitaph on his gravestone, paid for by former pupils, reads: 'In yonder sacred pile his voice was wont to sound, And now his body rests beneath the hallowed ground. He taught the peasant boy to read and use the pen; His earthly toils are o'er; he's cry'd his last Amen'.

NEWCHURCH, THE POST OFFICE c1955 N113004
Not far from Newchurch, in what was once the extensive forest of Bordwood, is a mound of earth called Queen Bower, from which it is said Isabella de Fortibus, Lady of the Island, watched the chase of the deer.

NEWPORT, MEDINA QUAY 1913 66327
This atmospheric photograph of the Medina at Newport gives some idea of the harbour at the height of its prosperity. At high tide, vessels of considerable size would make their way up from Cowes to unload and take on board a variety of merchandise.

NEWPORT, HIGH STREET 1892 30066
Newport is the commercial capital of the Isle of Wight, its ancient port still busily in use, five miles inland on the River Medina. Some historians have suggested that the town is Roman in origin, given its straight streets and regular layout.

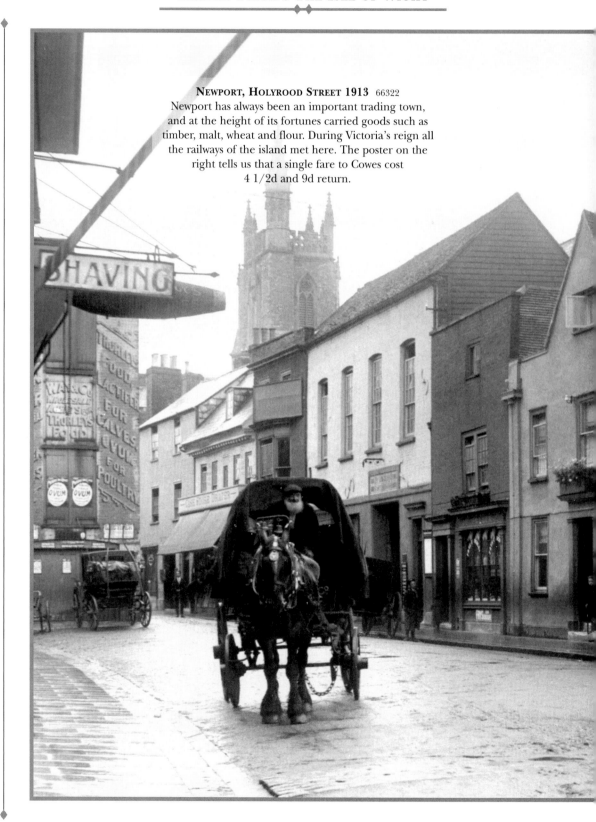

NEWPORT, HOLYROOD STREET 1913 66322
Newport has always been an important trading town,
and at the height of its fortunes carried goods such as
timber, malt, wheat and flour. During Victoria's reign all
the railways of the island met here. The poster on the
right tells us that a single fare to Cowes cost
4 1/2d and 9d return.

NEWPORT, ST JAMES SQUARE c1955 N24002

Three of Elizabeth Tudor's most influential courtiers hailed from Newport: Dr Edes, her chaplain, Dr James, her doctor, and Thomas Fleming, who became Lord Chief Justice. The witty monarch remarked that one was good for her soul, another for her body and the third for her goods.

NEWPORT, HIGH STREET c1955 N24003

Justice Fleming survived into the reign of James I, when he presided over the trial of Guy Fawkes; an act of judicial importance that is commemorated in Newport's Guildhall. Within the Town Hall, which once occupied the Guildhall site, Charles I negotiated with Parliament's Commissioners after his defeat in the Civil War.

NEWPORT, HIGH STREET c1955 N24004

Newport has many connections to famous people. Wellington, Canning and Palmerston represented the town in Parliament. John Keats wrote the first lines of 'Endymion' - 'A thing of beauty is a joy for ever' - nearby, and the Regency architect John Nash designed the town square and the Guildhall.

NEWPORT, ST JAMES SQUARE c1955 N24006

The amount of traffic in this photograph, even for a busy day in the 1950s, shows Newport's importance as a junction and central gathering point for the entire island - with public transport heading off to its furthest reaches.

NEWPORT, THE RIVER c1955 N24008

Newport's importance as a mercantile centre is shown here in this photograph of vessels loading and unloading on the banks of the Medina. All islands depend on the ease with which goods are imported and exported for their survival and prosperity. The sign on the large warehouse advertises a daily cargo boat to and from the mainland.

OSBORNE HOUSE 1893 32830

Osborne House was purchased by Queen Victoria in 1840, and it became something of a shrine to her beloved Prince Albert after his death. Victoria, Britain's longest serving monarch, died here on the evening of 22 January 1901 after a reign of 63 years, seven months and two days.

QUARR ABBEY, THE ABBEY C1875 8144

Quarr Abbey was probably named after the extensive quarries in the neighbourhood. The abbey was founded in 1132 by Baldwin de Redvers, afterwards Lord of the Island and Earl of Devon. After spending centuries as farm buildings, the abbey was restored by French monks early in the 20th century.

RYDE, THE PIER 1892 30033

Ryde is the nearest island port to the mainland, and a speedy crossing was usually guaranteed. In recent years the steamers so familiar to the Victorians have been replaced by faster ships and hovercrafts. Tourists can be met, as the photograph shows, by a convenient train or tram at the end of the pier.

RYDE, THE PIER c1883 16297
Ryde is one of the Isle of Wight's important access
ports, with ferries crossing the Solent each day. In
Victorian times steamers would take passengers on
long cruises from here around the entire island -
a very popular excursion.

RYDE, UNION STREET 1904 53165
Ryde is the Isle of Wight's largest holiday resort. Much of its architecture dates from the 19th century, a reminder that the Victorians made this island their own as a holiday and residential location. Union Street slopes steeply down to the sea front and its shops are a delight for browsing.

RYDE, THE PIER c1955 R76028

Sixty years after photograph No 30033 the half-mile long pier has changed very little. A few buildings have been demolished, there are some new additions, and only the remnants remain of the loading crane on the right. The biggest difference is the replacement of horsedrawn carriages with their horseless counterparts.

RYDE, UNION STREET 1913 66304

A fine view down the length of Union Street in the last peaceful days before the First World War. The shop awnings and broad-brimmed hats provide welcome relief from the glare of the sun as pedestrians stroll up and down to the seashore.

RYDE, UNION STREET 1904 53166
Henry Fielding, the 18th-century author of 'Tom Jones', called in at Ryde on his last journey to Lisbon. The novelist remarked on the beautiful setting of what was then just a straggling line of fishermen's cottages. Today's visitors still admire this attractive hillside town as they approach across the Solent.

RYDE, CROSS STREET c1955 R76031
A fishing settlement existed here from early times, the town being burnt by French raiders during the reign of Richard II. In Victorian times Ryde was occupied, in the stern words of one commentator, by '...a suburban population of retired officers and other more or less moneyed idlers'.

RYDE, UNION STREET C1955 R76029
Ryde is decorated here for its famous carnival held always at the beginning of September. A comparison with the earlier photographs shows a marked increase in traffic and the replacement of gas lamps with electric lighting.

RYDE, THE ESPLANADE 1918 68295

RYDE
The Esplanade 1918
In 1870 the Victorian yachtsman Sir John Burgoyne brought the Empress Eugenie of France to the town after a perilous channel crossing. Germany had defeated France at the Battle of Sedan and the Empress was forced to flee her homeland for ever. In later years she took up residence at a number of similar south coast resorts.

RYDE, THE ESPLANADE 1913 66302

Ryde's Esplanade conceals a tragic story. In 1782 the man-o-war 'Royal George' heeled over just offshore on a calm day. Seven hundred British sailors were drowned, probably because the officer of the watch would not believe that the ship was taking water. Many of those lost are buried under the present Esplanade.

RYDE, THE ESPLANADE 1927 80417

Victorian guide book writers were not impressed by the bathing at Ryde. 'The shallowness of the shore', one commented, 'may seem a merciful provision of nature to keep enterprising swimmers from venturing out too far, as there is a strong current to be reckoned with'.

RYDE, EASTERN GARDENS c1955 R76007

Given the difficulties with bathing, the sea front was given over to recreational use; it was a place to sit and relax, watch the ships in the Solent, hire a boat to explore the coastline or seek out the fine walks in the locality.

RYDE, THE ESPLANADE c1955 R76027
This view looks across the Solent from the Esplanade with the Ryde Esplanade station on the right. Notice the roller-skating rink in the middle of the photograph - an activity that became very popular in the 1950s.

SANDOWN, THE ESPLANADE 1895 36249
The Victorians, who were fond of such comparisons, compared the locality of Sandown to the Bay of Naples. The long Esplanade was very popular from the earliest days of the resort's history - note the 'Ladies Only' bathing machine below the pier.

SANDOWN, THE BEACH 1892 30048
Sandown and its twin resort of Shanklin, a couple of
miles to the south, are connected by a long promenade that winds around the curve of Shanklin Bay.
This part of the coast offers some of the safest bathing
on the Isle of Wight.

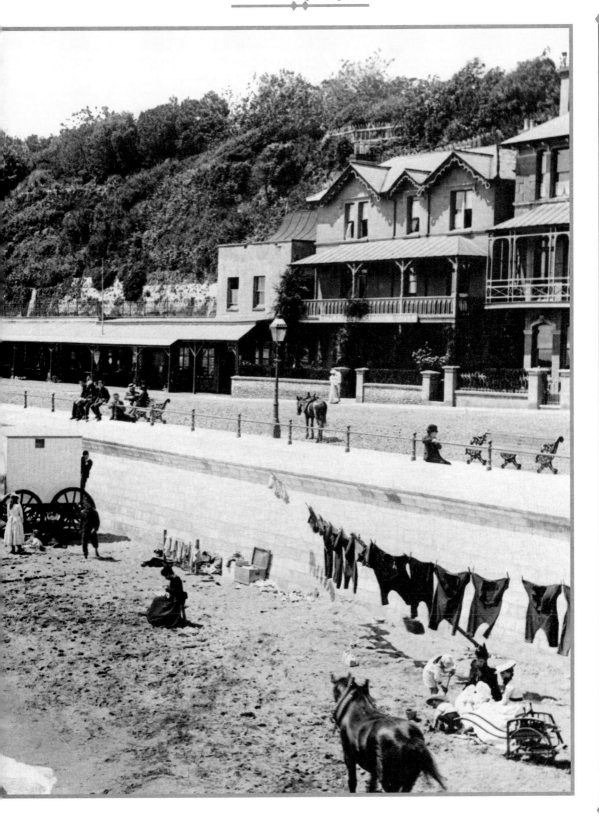

SANDOWN, THE PROMENADE 1895 36250

A fast rowing boat, a lobster pot and promenaders give an idea of how the Promenade looked in the last years of Victoria's reign. Sandown's leading hotels were very expensive at this time: even a room in a boarding house cost six shillings a day.

SANDOWN, THE STEPS 1908 60546

Given the Isle of Wight's popularity as a holiday and residential paradise, it comes as no surprise that the famous and well-to-do arrived at this charming resort. John Wilkes and David Garrick were early visitors, while Charles Darwin, Sir Isaac Pitman and Lewis Carroll spent long holidays here.

SANDOWN, THE BEACH 1918 68285

Behind the coastline are beautiful gardens and walks to attractive spots in the locality, such as Bembridge Down and the Culver Cliffs. Walking is one of the very best ways to explore the delights of the Isle of Wight.

SANDOWN, THE PIER C1951 S57020

Sandown's pier was originally built to allow steamers to come near to shore. The early structure fought a valiant battle against the worst of the channel storms, but managed to survive. When this photograph was taken Bill Scott Gordon's 'Revels of 1951' was the hit show at the pier theatre.

SANDOWN, THE PIER c1955 S57022
A stroll along the pier could be taken during the day, either for exercise or to catch a pleasure boat for a trip along the coast, or in the evening to take advantage of the dance hall - the Melotones provided the music when this photograph was taken.

SANDOWN
The Promenade c1955
The coastline on either side of Sandown was heavily fortified in earlier times, for fear of a French invasion was never far from English minds over several centuries. These days, happily, the only active defences to be found at the resort are sand castles on the beach.

SANDOWN, THE PROMENADE c1955 S57006

SANDOWN, THE BEACH AND PROMENADE c1955 S57021

Lines of hotels along the sea front testify to Sandown's continued popularity through the 20th century. Beach huts and bathing tents cater for those who love to bathe or just lie on the sands in the sunshine.

SANDOWN, HIGH STREET c1955 S57002

The Sandown we see today is mostly Victorian in origin, and most of the buildings are functional rather than decorative. Sandown's parish church is 19th century, though it has an imitation Norman doorway built in honour of Sir Henry Oglander, last of that famous Isle of Wight family, who died in 1874.

SANDOWN, HIGH STREET c1955 S57009
The original Sandown castle was built by Henry VIII but was destroyed by the sea. The Stuarts rebuilt the castle, but it had fallen into disrepair long before it was demolished in 1864, its stones being used for the Victorian fortifications.

SANDOWN, HIGH STREET c1955 S57010
The safe beaches and plentiful accommodation ensured Sandown's popularity as a family resort throughout the 20th century. Notice the very decorative lamp post on the right-hand side of the road.

Seaview, Suspension Bridge 1913 66340
The chain suspension bridge at the appropriately named Seaview leads out to the steamer landing stage. From here boats would arrive and depart on a daily basis to the mainland at Southsea.

Seaview
The Sands 1918
Seaview developed as a watering place in Victorian times. These tents enabled the modest to change with dignity. The woodlands in the distance, a rare example of trees coming down to the seashore, were both private and jealously guarded a century ago.

Seaview, The Sands 1918 68255

SEAVIEW, THE SEA FRONT 1918 68263

Seaview shows off a huge variety of architecture, as this photograph demonstrates. Its buildings are both picturesque and smart and have obviously developed at the whim of individual owners, rather than uniformly as with some other towns on the Isle of Wight.

SEAVIEW, HIGH STREET 1918 68264

The narrow streets of Seaview tell us that this is an old settlement. Seaview was a renowned fishing village when the French made their unsuccessful attempt at invasion in 1545.

SEAVIEW, SEAFIELD ROAD 1918 68266
Before the availability of cars, visitors would explore the Isle of Wight in a variety of ways - perhaps on foot or bicycle in combination with the island's excellent rail network. Here we see a charabanc on a day excursion with a full load of passengers - a popular way to see the sights.

SEAVIEW, WEST STREET 1918 68265
The walk eastward along the coast from Ryde was a favourite excursion for Victorian ramblers, who admired the fine scenery along the way. The round trip was about seven miles, though foot-weary visitors could refresh themselves at inns along the way.

SEAVIEW, HIGH STREET 1918 68268

SEAVIEW
High Street 1918
A view of Seaview's High Street during the final summer of the First World War. The lady on the right demonstrates the changing fashions caused by the shortage of materials. Such a high hemline would have been considered very daring a decade before.

SEAVIEW, SALTERNS COTTAGES 1918 68271

The name 'saltern' suggests that this was a place where early inhabitants of the island would come to the seashore in search of salt for the winter preservation of meat. These cottages probably stand on the site of the original settlement at Seaview.

SHALFLEET, THE VILLAGE c1955 S496014

On the busy Yarmouth road, Shalfleet is renowned for the splendour of its Norman church tower, the oldest on the island. Early in the 20th century the tower's foundations had to be re-laid in concrete after it was discovered that only ten feet of clay and water were holding up the structure.

SHALFLEET, THE VILLAGE c1955 S496011

The attractive cottages at Shalfleet are a delight to the eye, several being hundreds of years old. The post office and stores on the left is as old as any other local building, but its rooftop boasts an innovation soon to spread across the rooftops of most houses on the Isle of Wight - a television aerial.

SHALFLEET, NEW INN c1955 S496021

Sea scouts share in this idle scene outside the local public house on a sunny day half a century ago. The New Inn has been the focus of community life in Shalfleet since Victorian times.

SHANKLIN, THE BEACH 1893 32852

Safe bathing brought thousands of early visitors to Shanklin, as we can see from the profusion of bathing huts and tents. Many of the boats in the foreground would have been for hire. Victorian holidaymakers of some competence were encouraged to explore the coastline of Shanklin Bay by boat.

SHANKLIN, THE PARADE 1908 60562

Ladies promenade all dressed in fine examples of Edwardian fashion, with parasols to protect those 'pale and interesting' complexions from the fierce rays of the sun. A long line of purpose-built hotels and boarding houses cater for the visitors to this much-frequented watering place.

SHANKLIN, THE PARADE 1908 60560
A newer Shanklin grew up along the seashore to cater
for the demands of both visitors and those who came
to settle. The pier, seen here on the left, was described
by one Victorian tourist as 'a pretentious structure, a
little out of keeping with the tone of the place'.

SHANKLIN, THE VILLAGE 1896 37239
At the inland end of Shanklin Chine is the old village, a delightful array of thatched cottages, with honeysuckle and roses around the door. The place is as attractive today as it was in this old photograph.

SHANKLIN, ENTRANCE TO THE CHINE 1913 66206
Shanklin Chine is a geological fissure in the cliffs, with a spectacular ravine and pretty waterfall. By Victorian times it had been transformed into a tea garden of some renown, on the itinerary of all visitors to the Isle of Wight.

SHANKLIN, APPLEY CLIFFS BATHING TENTS 1918 68293
A good bathing day beneath Appley Cliffs, which give shelter to Shanklin's southern beaches. A very steep climb leads up the cliffs above the line of bathing tents. When the tide is out it is possible to walk a long way along the shoreline.

SHANKLIN, THE STAGECOACHES 1913 66211A
Stagecoaches, remnants of a bygone age even in 1913, take tourists on local excursions. Notice the man with the stepladder, evidently used to enable passengers to ascend to the top of the coach. Nearby a photographer struggles with his camera.

SHANKLIN, THE BEACH 1918 68292

Two poets who admired Shanklin were Longfellow and Keats. The latter write his poem 'Lamia' here, while Longfellow wrote a verse in praise of the ferruginous spring which issues out of the Chine, whose waters health-conscious visitors came to sample.

SHANKLIN, THE PIER 1927 80456

This photograph gives an excellent view over Shanklin sea front and pier, with the sands filled with bathers, boats, tents and bathing machines. Charabancs are drawn up by the clock tower to convey tourists around the island.

SHORWELL
The Water Wheel c1955
In the days before electricity and gas power was supplied, the water wheel was a simple but very effective invention for powering mills serving a variety of functions.

SHORWELL, THE WATER WHEEL AT YAFFORD C1955 S414317

SHORWELL, THE VILLAGE 1951 S414007
Situated amongst beautiful woodland, the inland village of Shorwell was one of Queen Victoria's favourite excursions on the Isle of Wight. It is said that she often made the journey here from Osborne House to admire the setting of this village and its fascinating old church.

SHORWELL, ST PETER'S CHURCH c1955 S414021

Inside the church is a fine memorial to Sir John Leigh, who died in 1629. His nine-month-old grandson died before Sir John could be buried. They now share a tomb and epitaph: 'Inmate in grave, he took his grandchild heir, Whose soul did haste to make to him repair, And so to heaven along as little page With him did post, to wait upon his age.'

ST HELENS, THE GREEN c1955 S514014

St Helens overlooks the tidal creeks above Brading Harbour. Many come to admire the broad village green, the leafy lanes and nearby woodland. There are places to explore, or you can just sit quietly and admire the scenery.

TOTLAND BAY, THE BAY AND THE PIER 1892 30077
Totland Bay is the westernmost inhabited bay on the Isle of Wight, with views up the English Channel to Bournemouth and the Dorset coast. This resort was established in Victorian times and quickly found favour with eminent visitors such as Alfred, Lord Tennyson and the Queen herself.

TOTLAND BAY, THE PIER 1897 40385
A writer who visited Totland Bay at around the time this photograph was taken said 'Totland Bay is a rising watering place, all new and smart, with its big hotel standing out over the pier like the captain of a company of red brick villas'.

TOTLAND BAY, THE BEACH c1955 T65009

TOTLAND BAY
The Beach c1955
Totland Bay is a good starting point for a long coastal ramble past The Needles to Alum Bay - some of the most dramatic coastal scenery in England. The less energetic can laze on a deckchair, hire a beach hut and watch the world go by.

◆

TOTLAND BAY
The Broadway c1955
In the last years of the 19th century Marconi set up an early wireless transmitting station near to Totland Bay, exchanging radio signals with a steamer out at sea. In 1898 the first paid Marconigram - an early form of telegram - was transmitted from this station.

TOTLAND BAY, THE BROADWAY c1955 T65017

VENTNOR, THE BEACH 1899 43133
Ventnor transformed itself from an obscure fishing hamlet to a fashionable watering place during the last half of the 19th century. The eminent physician Sir James Clark made the resort's reputation in Victorian times by comparing its climate to that of Madeira.

VENTNOR, THE ESPLANADE 1892 30061

A sheltered location and mild climate have brought generations of holidaymakers to Ventnor. The town lies at the foot of an eight hundred feet hill with gradients in some streets of 1 in 4. This shelter aids the growth of luxuriant vegetation in the steep gardens.

VENTNOR, THE BEACH 1899 43138

Victorian Ventnor became a refuge for consumptives, the kind climate aiding their condition. In a few short years four large homes for sufferers from tuberculosis were established in the resort. The good weather, fresh air and regime of long bracing walks probably did a great deal to alleviate their condition.

VENTNOR, THE ESPLANADE 1908 60527
Ventnor never compared to Sandown or Shanklin as a centre for sea bathing, though bathing machines for ladies and gentlemen flourished in King Edward VII's reign. Bowling greens, tennis courts, concert shows and walks were provided for those too nervous to dip a toe in to the cool waters of the English Channel.

VENTNOR, THE STATION 1908 60534
Victorian enthusiasm for railways soon ensured that all the major tourist centres of the Isle of Wight could be reached by the Permanent Way. Visitors would often combine the use of a train with cycling or walking as a way of seeing the island.

VENTNOR, FROM THE CLIFFS 1918 68280
This panoramic view over Ventnor gives an idea of the steepness of the town. As one Victorian commented, 'nature never meant herself here to be laid out in streets, and eligible plots of building land have to be taken as they can be found on the steep slopes'.

VENTNOR, THE CHILDREN'S CORNER 1913 66160
Children play with their toy yachts in the dedicated Children's Corner at Ventnor. In the background promenaders walk past a prominent establishment offering hot and cold sea water baths.

WHIPPINGHAM, THE CHURCH c1955 W79001
Whippingham village lies close to Osborne House, and Victoria's consort Prince Albert had a hand in the extraordinary design of the church. In the churchyard lie the remains of many of the Queen's servants, their memorials raised at her expense.

WHITWELL, THE VILLAGE c1955 W467001
Whitwell's church was restored in 1868, but is several centuries older, with a Tudor porch and tower. A small statue of Joan of Arc commemorates the men of Whitwell who did not return from the Great War.

WHITWELL, THE POST OFFICE c1955 W467004
Whitwell's church once served two parishes, the building being divided in half by a stone wall. This was opened up by an archway in the 16th century, and the church then became just one place of worship.

WOOTTON BRIDGE, THE BRIDGE c1955 W282001
For centuries a strong tide has swept up Wootton Creek to work the ancient mill - one of the very few tidally-powered mills in the world. Not far away from Osborne House, Wootton was another of Queen Victoria's favourite excursions.

WOOTTON BRIDGE, THE SLOOP INN c1955 W282011
Wootton Bridge has many connections with the sea, as the name of its inn suggests. In the churchyard lies the grave of the Victorian admiral Sir John Baird, who died in 1908. His tomb bears an anchor tied to a cross with the epitaph 'And so He bringeth them into the haven where they would be'.

WOOTTON BRIDGE
High Street c1955
Wootton has one of the oldest churches on the Isle of Wight, being built originally by the Lisle family who took their name - De L'ile - from their island residence.

YARMOUTH
The Bugle Inn 1923
Yarmouth is an excellent centre for exploring the western half of the Isle of Wight, with Totland and Alum Bays and the Needles being not far away. A dramatic causeway leads across the mouth of the River Yar to the many attractions of the Freshwater peninsula.

WOOTTON BRIDGE, HIGH STREET c1955 W282015

YARMOUTH, THE BUGLE INN 1923 74740

YARMOUTH, THE SQUARE c1960 Y4016
Yarmouth has become an important entry port to the Isle of Wight due to ease of access from the mainland. It is no longer 'the sleepy old place of less than a thousand inhabitants that can boast to have seen better days' as noted by a guidebook writer of the 1890s.

YARMOUTH, THE SQUARE c1955 Y4003
Yarmouth's church was built between 1611 and 1614, and restored by the Victorians in 1873. Within is the impressive tomb of the Caroleon admiral Sir Robert Holmes. If the head on his effigy does not quite seem to match the body, that is because it was added later. The admiral captured a statue of Louis IV on a French vessel, and thought it would be ideal for his own monument. He paid a sculptor to add a new head.

YARMOUTH
Bridge Road c1955

Yarmouth's original church was fired by the French raiders who twice attacked the town. Its castle, one of four block-houses built by Henry VIII, was garrisoned until Victorian times, such was the prolonged fear of invasion from across the channel.

◆

YARMOUTH
The Bugle Hotel c1955

Although Yarmouth never really developed as a traditional seaside resort, there are stretches of sand available for bathing. Its accessibility to the mainland and its usefulness as a touring centre ensured that a number of fine hotels, such as the Bugle, were opened from Victorian times onwards.

YARMOUTH, BRIDGE ROAD c1955 Y4011

YARMOUTH, THE BUGLE HOTEL c1955 Y4021

YARMOUTH, QUAY STREET c1955 Y4022

Quay Street is one of the oldest parts of Yarmouth, and must have been familiar to the generations of seamen who frequented its inns. The George Hotel, here on the right, offered popular accommodation to Victorian visitors and those who came this way throughout the 20th century.

YARMOUTH, THE QUAY c1955 Y4008

A strange tale relates how many of the ancient charters of the town were lost for ever. A ship's captain, drunk after a Court Leet dinner in 1784, stole what he thought was a case of wine as he returned to his ship. When he discovered that the case was full of books, he threw them overboard, consigning many of Yarmouth's historical records to the bottom of the sea.

YARMOUTH, THE HARBOUR c1955 Y4032
There are few scenes on the Isle of Wight more captivating than Yarmouth harbour on a busy sailing day. Boats of the Solent Yacht Club often set out from here, and vessels of all descriptions seek shelter from the channel gales.

YARMOUTH, THE PIER c1955 Y4002
Yarmouth's pier is functional rather than decorative, a place to fish or simply to sit and watch the mainland ferries. It was built originally as a landing stage for local boats and ships.

YARMOUTH, THE FERRY c1955 Y4010

YARMOUTH
The Ferry c1955
The ferry from the mainland prepares to dock and unload its cargo of motor vehicles and foot passengers. The vessel crosses from Lymington in Hampshire, and offers one of the shortest passages across the Solent.

YARMOUTH
The Ferry c1955
Passengers disembark for their holiday on the Isle of Wight. Many return - as Queen Victoria did - year after year. Exploring the dramatic coastline, pastoral countryside and delightful towns and villages never fails to make for a memorable holiday.

YARMOUTH, THE FERRY c1955 Y4019

Index

Frith Book Co Titles

www.francisfrith.co.uk

The Frith Book Company publishes over 100 new titles each year. A selection of those currently available is listed below. For latest catalogue please contact Frith Book Co.
Town Books 96 pages, approximately 100 photos. **County and Themed Books** 128 pages, approximately 150 photos (unless specified). All titles hardback with laminated case and jacket, except those indicated pb (paperback)

Amersham, Chesham & Rickmansworth (pb)	1-85937-340-2	£9.99	Devon (pb)	1-85937-297-x	£9.99
Andover (pb)	1-85937-292-9	£9.99	Devon Churches (pb)	1-85937-250-3	£9.99
Aylesbury (pb)	1-85937-227-9	£9.99	Dorchester (pb)	1-85937-307-0	£9.99
Barnstaple (pb)	1-85937-300-3	£9.99	Dorset (pb)	1-85937-269-4	£9.99
Basildon Living Memories (pb)	1-85937-515-4	£9.99	Dorset Coast (pb)	1-85937-299-6	£9.99
Bath (pb)	1-85937-419-0	£9.99	Dorset Living Memories (pb)	1-85937-584-7	£9.99
Bedford (pb)	1-85937-205-8	£9.99	Down the Severn (pb)	1-85937-560-x	£9.99
Bedfordshire Living Memories	1-85937-513-8	£14.99	Down The Thames (pb)	1-85937-278-3	£9.99
Belfast (pb)	1-85937-303-8	£9.99	Down the Trent	1-85937-311-9	£14.99
Berkshire (pb)	1-85937-191-4	£9.99	East Anglia (pb)	1-85937-265-1	£9.99
Berkshire Churches	1-85937-170-1	£17.99	East Grinstead (pb)	1-85937-138-8	£9.99
Berkshire Living Memories	1-85937-332-1	£14.99	East London	1-85937-080-2	£14.99
Black Country	1-85937-497-2	£12.99	East Sussex (pb)	1-85937-606-1	£9.99
Blackpool (pb)	1-85937-393-3	£9.99	Eastbourne (pb)	1-85937-399-2	£9.99
Bognor Regis (pb)	1-85937-431-x	£9.99	Edinburgh (pb)	1-85937-193-0	£8.99
Bournemouth (pb)	1-85937-545-6	£9.99	England In The 1880s	1-85937-331-3	£17.99
Bradford (pb)	1-85937-204-x	£9.99	Essex - Second Selection	1-85937-456-5	£14.99
Bridgend (pb)	1-85937-386-0	£7.99	Essex (pb)	1-85937-270-8	£9.99
Bridgwater (pb)	1-85937-305-4	£9.99	Essex Coast	1-85937-342-9	£14.99
Bridport (pb)	1-85937-327-5	£9.99	Essex Living Memories	1-85937-490-5	£14.99
Brighton (pb)	1-85937-192-2	£8.99	Exeter	1-85937-539-1	£9.99
Bristol (pb)	1-85937-264-3	£9.99	Exmoor (pb)	1-85937-608-8	£9.99
British Life A Century Ago (pb)	1-85937-213-9	£9.99	Falmouth (pb)	1-85937-594-4	£9.99
Buckinghamshire (pb)	1-85937-200-7	£9.99	Folkestone (pb)	1-85937-124-8	£9.99
Camberley (pb)	1-85937-222-8	£9.99	Frome (pb)	1-85937-317-8	£9.99
Cambridge (pb)	1-85937-422-0	£9.99	Glamorgan	1-85937-488-3	£14.99
Cambridgeshire (pb)	1-85937-420-4	£9.99	Glasgow (pb)	1-85937-190-6	£9.99
Cambridgeshire Villages	1-85937-523-5	£14.99	Glastonbury (pb)	1-85937-338-0	£7.99
Canals And Waterways (pb)	1-85937-291-0	£9.99	Gloucester (pb)	1-85937-232-5	£9.99
Canterbury Cathedral (pb)	1-85937-179-5	£9.99	Gloucestershire (pb)	1-85937-561-8	£9.99
Cardiff (pb)	1-85937-093-4	£9.99	Great Yarmouth (pb)	1-85937-426-3	£9.99
Carmarthenshire (pb)	1-85937-604-5	£9.99	Greater Manchester (pb)	1-85937-266-x	£9.99
Chelmsford (pb)	1-85937-310-0	£9.99	Guildford (pb)	1-85937-410-7	£9.99
Cheltenham (pb)	1-85937-095-0	£9.99	Hampshire (pb)	1-85937-279-1	£9.99
Cheshire (pb)	1-85937-271-6	£9.99	Harrogate (pb)	1-85937-423-9	£9.99
Chester (pb)	1-85937-382 8	£9.99	Hastings and Bexhill (pb)	1-85937-131-0	£9.99
Chesterfield (pb)	1-85937-378-x	£9.99	Heart of Lancashire (pb)	1-85937-197-3	£9.99
Chichester (pb)	1-85937-228-7	£9.99	Helston (pb)	1-85937-214-7	£9.99
Churches of East Cornwall (pb)	1-85937-249-x	£9.99	Hereford (pb)	1-85937-175-2	£9.99
Churches of Hampshire (pb)	1-85937-207-4	£9.99	Herefordshire (pb)	1-85937-567-7	£9.99
Cinque Ports & Two Ancient Towns	1-85937-492-1	£14.99	Herefordshire Living Memories	1-85937-514-6	£14.99
Colchester (pb)	1-85937-188-4	£8.99	Hertfordshire (pb)	1-85937-247-3	£9.99
Cornwall (pb)	1-85937-229-5	£9.99	Horsham (pb)	1-85937-432-8	£9.99
Cornwall Living Memories	1-85937-248-1	£14.99	Humberside (pb)	1-85937-605-3	£9.99
Cotswolds (pb)	1-85937-230-9	£9.99	Hythe, Romney Marsh, Ashford (pb)	1-85937-256-2	£9.99
Cotswolds Living Memories	1-85937-255-4	£14.99	Ipswich (pb)	1-85937-424-7	£9.99
County Durham (pb)	1-85937-398-4	£9.99	Isle of Man (pb)	1-85937-268-6	£9.99
Croydon Living Memories (pb)	1-85937-162-0	£9.99	Isle of Wight (pb)	1-85937-429-8	£9.99
Cumbria (pb)	1-85937-621-5	£9.99	Isle of Wight Living Memories	1-85937-304-6	£14.99
Derby (pb)	1-85937-367-4	£9.99	Kent (pb)	1-85937-189-2	£9.99
Derbyshire (pb)	1-85937-196-5	£9.99	Kent Living Memories(pb)	1-85937-401-8	£9.99
Derbyshire Living Memories	1-85937-330-5	£14.99	Kings Lynn (pb)	1-85937-334-8	£9.99

Available from your local bookshop or from the publisher

Frith Book Co Titles (continued)

Lake District (pb)	1-85937-275-9	£9.99
Lancashire Living Memories	1-85937-335-6	£14.99
Lancaster, Morecambe, Heysham (pb)	1-85937-233-3	£9.99
Leeds (pb)	1-85937-202-3	£9.99
Leicester (pb)	1-85937-381-x	£9.99
Leicestershire & Rutland Living Memories	1-85937-500-6	£12.99
Leicestershire (pb)	1-85937-185-x	£9.99
Lighthouses	1-85937-257-0	£9.99
Lincoln (pb)	1-85937-380-1	£9.99
Lincolnshire (pb)	1-85937-433-6	£9.99
Liverpool and Merseyside (pb)	1-85937-234-1	£9.99
London (pb)	1-85937-183-3	£9.99
London Living Memories	1-85937-454-9	£14.99
Ludlow (pb)	1-85937-176-0	£9.99
Luton (pb)	1-85937-235-x	£9.99
Maidenhead (pb)	1-85937-339-9	£9.99
Maidstone (pb)	1-85937-391-7	£9.99
Manchester (pb)	1-85937-198-1	£9.99
Marlborough (pb)	1-85937-336-4	£9.99
Middlesex	1-85937-158-2	£14.99
Monmouthshire	1-85937-532-4	£14.99
New Forest (pb)	1-85937-390-9	£9.99
Newark (pb)	1-85937-366-6	£9.99
Newport, Wales (pb)	1-85937-258-9	£9.99
Newquay (pb)	1-85937-421-2	£9.99
Norfolk (pb)	1-85937-195-7	£9.99
Norfolk Broads	1-85937-486-7	£14.99
Norfolk Living Memories (pb)	1-85937-402-6	£9.99
North Buckinghamshire	1-85937-626-6	£14.99
North Devon Living Memories	1-85937-261-9	£14.99
North Hertfordshire	1-85937-547-2	£14.99
North London (pb)	1-85937-403-4	£9.99
North Somerset	1-85937-302-x	£14.99
North Wales (pb)	1-85937-298-8	£9.99
North Yorkshire (pb)	1-85937-236-8	£9.99
Northamptonshire Living Memories	1-85937-529-4	£14.99
Northamptonshire	1-85937-150-7	£14.99
Northumberland Tyne & Wear (pb)	1-85937-281-3	£9.99
Northumberland	1-85937-522-7	£14.99
Norwich (pb)	1-85937-194-9	£8.99
Nottingham (pb)	1-85937-324-0	£9.99
Nottinghamshire (pb)	1-85937-187-6	£9.99
Oxford (pb)	1-85937-411-5	£9.99
Oxfordshire (pb)	1-85937-430-1	£9.99
Oxfordshire Living Memories	1-85937-525-1	£14.99
Paignton (pb)	1-85937-374-7	£7.99
Peak District (pb)	1-85937-280-5	£9.99
Pembrokeshire	1-85937-262-7	£14.99
Penzance (pb)	1-85937-595-2	£9.99
Peterborough (pb)	1-85937-219-8	£9.99
Picturesque Harbours	1-85937-208-2	£14.99
Piers	1-85937-237-6	£17.99
Plymouth (pb)	1-85937-389-5	£9.99
Poole & Sandbanks (pb)	1-85937-251-1	£9.99
Preston (pb)	1-85937-212-0	£9.99
Reading (pb)	1-85937-238-4	£9.99
Redhill to Reigate (pb)	1-85937-596-0	£9.99
Ringwood (pb)	1-85937-384-4	£7.99
Romford (pb)	1-85937-319-4	£9.99
Royal Tunbridge Wells (pb)	1-85937-504-9	£9.99
Salisbury (pb)	1-85937-239-2	£9.99
Scarborough (pb)	1-85937-379-8	£9.99
Sevenoaks and Tonbridge (pb)	1-85937-392-5	£9.99
Sheffield & South Yorks (pb)	1-85937-267-8	£9.99
Sherborne (pb)	1-85937-301-1	£9.99
Shrewsbury (pb)	1-85937-325-9	£9.99
Shropshire (pb)	1-85937-326-7	£9.99
Shropshire Living Memories	1-85937-643-6	£14.99
Somerset	1-85937-153-1	£14.99
South Devon Coast	1-85937-107-8	£14.99
South Devon Living Memories (pb)	1-85937-609-6	£9.99
South East London (pb)	1-85937-263-5	£9.99
South Somerset	1-85937-318-6	£14.99
South Wales	1-85937-519-7	£14.99
Southampton (pb)	1-85937-427-1	£9.99
Southend (pb)	1-85937-313-5	£9.99
Southport (pb)	1-85937-425-5	£9.99
St Albans (pb)	1-85937-341-0	£9.99
St Ives (pb)	1-85937-415-8	£9.99
Stafford Living Memories (pb)	1-85937-503-0	£9.99
Staffordshire (pb)	1-85937-308-9	£9.99
Stourbridge (pb)	1-85937-530-8	£9.99
Stratford upon Avon (pb)	1-85937-388-7	£9.99
Suffolk (pb)	1-85937-221-x	£9.99
Suffolk Coast (pb)	1-85937-610-x	£9.99
Surrey (pb)	1-85937-240-6	£9.99
Surrey Living Memories	1-85937-328-3	£14.99
Sussex (pb)	1-85937-184-1	£9.99
Sutton (pb)	1-85937-337-2	£9.99
Swansea (pb)	1-85937-167-1	£9.99
Taunton (pb)	1-85937-314-3	£9.99
Tees Valley & Cleveland (pb)	1-85937-623-1	£9.99
Teignmouth (pb)	1-85937-370-4	£7.99
Thanet (pb)	1-85937-116-7	£9.99
Tiverton (pb)	1-85937-178-7	£9.99
Torbay (pb)	1-85937-597-9	£9.99
Truro (pb)	1-85937-598-7	£9.99
Victorian & Edwardian Dorset	1-85937-254-6	£14.99
Victorian & Edwardian Kent (pb)	1-85937-624-X	£9.99
Victorian & Edwardian Maritime Album (pb)	1-85937-622-3	£9.99
Victorian and Edwardian Sussex (pb)	1-85937-625-8	£9.99
Villages of Devon (pb)	1-85937-293-7	£9.99
Villages of Kent (pb)	1-85937-294-5	£9.99
Villages of Sussex (pb)	1-85937-295-3	£9.99
Warrington (pb)	1-85937-507-3	£9.99
Warwick (pb)	1-85937-518-9	£9.99
Warwickshire (pb)	1-85937-203-1	£9.99
Welsh Castles (pb)	1-85937-322-4	£9.99
West Midlands (pb)	1-85937-289-9	£9.99
West Sussex (pb)	1-85937-607-x	£9.99
West Yorkshire (pb)	1-85937-201-5	£9.99
Weston Super Mare (pb)	1-85937-306-2	£9.99
Weymouth (pb)	1-85937-209-0	£9.99
Wiltshire (pb)	1-85937-277-5	£9.99
Wiltshire Churches (pb)	1-85937-171-x	£9.99
Wiltshire Living Memories (pb)	1-85937-396-8	£9.99
Winchester (pb)	1-85937-428-x	£9.99
Windsor (pb)	1-85937-333-x	£9.99
Wokingham & Bracknell (pb)	1-85937-329-1	£9.99
Woodbridge (pb)	1-85937-498-0	£9.99
Worcester (pb)	1-85937-165-5	£9.99
Worcestershire Living Memories	1-85937-489-1	£14.99
Worcestershire	1-85937-152-3	£14.99
York (pb)	1-85937-199-x	£9.99
Yorkshire (pb)	1-85937-186-8	£9.99
Yorkshire Coastal Memories	1-85937-506-5	£14.99
Yorkshire Dales	1-85937-502-2	£14.99
Yorkshire Living Memories (pb)	1-85937-397-6	£9.99

See Frith books on the internet at www.francisfrith.co.uk

FRITH PRODUCTS & SERVICES

Francis Frith would doubtless be pleased to know that the pioneering publishing venture he started in 1860 still continues today. Over a hundred and forty years later, The Francis Frith Collection continues in the same innovative tradition and is now one of the foremost publishers of vintage photographs in the world. Some of the current activities include:

Interior Decoration

Today Frith's photographs can be seen framed and as giant wall murals in thousands of pubs, restaurants, hotels, banks, retail stores and other public buildings throughout the country. In every case they enhance the unique local atmosphere of the places they depict and provide reminders of gentler days in an increasingly busy and frenetic world.

Product Promotions

Frith products are used by many major companies to promote the sales of their own products or to reinforce their own history and heritage. Frith promotions have been used by Hovis bread, Courage beers, Scots Porage Oats, Colman's mustard, Cadbury's foods, Mellow Birds coffee, Dunhill pipe tobacco, Guinness, and Bulmer's Cider.

Genealogy and Family History

As the interest in family history and roots grows world-wide, more and more people are turning to Frith's photographs of Great Britain for images of the towns, villages and streets where their ancestors lived; and, of course, photographs of the churches and chapels where their ancestors were christened, married and buried are an essential part of every genealogy tree and family album.

Frith Products

All Frith photographs are available Framed or just as Mounted Prints and Posters (size 23 x 16 inches). These may be ordered from the address below. From time to time other products - Address Books, Calendars, Table Mats, etc - are available.

The Internet

Already fifty thousand Frith photographs can be viewed and purchased on the internet through the Frith websites and a myriad of partner sites.

For more detailed information on Frith companies and products, look at these sites:

www.francisfrith.co.uk
www.francisfrith.com
(for North American visitors)

See the complete list of Frith Books at:

www.francisfrith.co.uk

This web site is regularly updated with the latest list of publications from the Frith Book Company. If you wish to buy books relating to another part of the country that your local bookshop does not stock, you may purchase on-line.

For further information, trade, or author enquiries please contact us at the address below:
The Francis Frith Collection, Frith's Barn, Teffont, Salisbury, Wiltshire, England SP3 5QP.
Tel: +44 (0)1722 716 376 Fax: +44 (0)1722 716 881 Email: sales@francisfrith.co.uk

See Frith books on the internet at www.francisfrith.co.uk

FREE MOUNTED PRINT

Mounted Print
Overall size 14 x 11 inches

Fill in and cut out this voucher and return
it with your remittance for £2.25 (to cover postage and handling). Offer valid for delivery to UK addresses only.

Choose any photograph included in this book.
Your SEPIA print will be A4 in size. It will be mounted in a cream mount with a burgundy rule line (overall size 14 x 11 inches).

**Order additional Mounted Prints
at HALF PRICE (only £7.49 each*)**
If you would like to order more Frith prints from this book, possibly as gifts for friends and family, you can buy them at half price (with no additional postage and handling costs).

Have your Mounted Prints framed
For an extra £14.95 per print* you can have your mounted print(s) framed in an elegant polished wood and gilt moulding, overall size 16 x 13 inches (no additional postage and handling required).

---

* IMPORTANT!

These special prices are only available if you order at the same time as you order your free mounted print. You must use the ORIGINAL VOUCHER on this page (no copies permitted). We can only despatch to one address.

Send completed Voucher form to:
The Francis Frith Collection, Frith's Barn, Teffont, Salisbury, Wiltshire SP3 5QP

Voucher *for FREE and Reduced Price Frith Prints*

Please do not photocopy this voucher. Only the original is valid, so please fill it in, cut it out and return it to us with your order.

Picture ref no	Page no	Qty	Mounted @ £7.49	Framed + £14.95	Total Cost
		1	Free of charge*	£	£
			£7.49	£	£
			£7.49	£	£
			£7.49	£	£
			£7.49	£	£
			£7.49	£	£

Please allow 28 days for delivery	* Post & handling (UK)	£2.25
	Total Order Cost	£

Title of this book . . . .

I enclose a cheque/postal order for £ . . . .
made payable to 'The Francis Frith Collection'

OR please debit my Mastercard / Visa / Switch / Amex card
(credit cards please on all overseas orders), details below

Card Number

Issue No (Switch only)   Valid from (Amex/Switch)

Expires   Signature

Name Mr/Mrs/Ms . . . .

Address . . . .

. . . .

. . . .

. . . . Postcode . . . .

Daytime Tel No . . . .

Email . . . .

Valid to 31/12/05

Free Print – see overleaf

Would you like to find out more about Francis Frith?

We have recently recruited some entertaining speakers who are happy to visit local groups, clubs and societies to give an illustrated talk documenting Frith's travels and photographs. If you are a member of such a group and are interested in hosting a presentation, we would love to hear from you.

Our speakers bring with them a small selection of our local town and county books, together with sample prints. They are happy to take orders. A small proportion of the order value is donated to the group who have hosted the presentation. The talks are therefore an excellent way of fundraising for small groups and societies.

Can you help us with information about any of the Frith photographs in this book?

We are gradually compiling an historical record for each of the photographs in the Frith archive. It is always fascinating to find out the names of the people shown in the pictures, as well as insights into the shops, buildings and other features depicted.

If you recognize anyone in the photographs in this book, or if you have information not already included in the author's caption, do let us know. We would love to hear from you, and will try to publish it in future books or articles.

Our production team

Frith books are produced by a small dedicated team at offices in the converted Grade II listed 18th-century barn at Teffont near Salisbury, illustrated above. Most have worked with the Frith Collection for many years. All have in common one quality: they have a passion for the Frith Collection. The team is constantly expanding, but currently includes:

Jason Buck, John Buck, Douglas Mitchell-Burns, Ruth Butler, Heather Crisp, Isobel Hall, Julian Hight, Peter Horne, James Kinnear, Karen Kinnear, Tina Leary, David Marsh, Sue Molloy, Kate Rotondetto, Dean Scource, Eliza Sackett, Terence Sackett, Sandra Sampson, Adrian Sanders, Sandra Sanger, Julia Skinner, Lewis Taylor, Shelley Tolcher and Lorraine Tuck.